OCEAN
Emporium

First published in Great Britain 2018 by Red Shed,
an imprint of Egmont UK Limited
The Yellow Building, 1 Nicholas Road, London W11 4AN

www.egmont.co.uk

Text copyright © Egmont UK Limited 2018

Illustrations copyright © Dawn Cooper 2018

ISBN 978 1 4052 9097 5

Consultancy by John Woodward.

A CIP catalogue record for this book is available from the British Library.

OCEAN
Emporium

Written by Susie Brooks
Illustrated by Dawn Cooper

RED SHED

Contents

Welcome to the Emporium

Deep, mysterious oceans sweep across our planet, making up 99 per cent of the living space on Earth. Beneath their rolling waves lies an extraordinary web of life, where colourful creatures great and small depend on each other to survive.

Small fish

Small fish often strive to protect themselves from predators by swimming in shoals, or schools.

Octopus

An octopus is an adept hunter, able to break into shells for food or paralyse fish prey with its toxic saliva.

Krill

These tiny crustaceans feed on plankton, and in turn are devoured in swarms by larger animals.

Plankton

Most marine life depends on these tiny plants and animals, which drift on ocean currents as they cannot swim.

Shellfish

Many marine molluscs live in shells, and feed by sifting plankton from the water.

Large fish

In the open ocean, even large fish must beware of seabirds, sharks, toothed whales and other predators.

Sharks

The fiercest sharks, such as the great white, are apex predators with most other sea life at their mercy.

Whales

Amazingly, vast humpbacks and other baleen whales survive primarily on feasts of tiny krill.

There may be more than a million species living in the world's oceans. They vary incredibly, from the largest animal that ever existed to creatures too small for the human eye to see. While some duck and dive in sunlit surface waters, others lurk thousands of metres below in the pitch-black abyss. Prepare to discover their amazing world as you plunge into the Ocean Emporium!

Corals

Corals are very much alive. They are made up of soft-bodied organisms called polyps, which feed on plankton.

Crabs

These active animals scuttle sideways under helmet-style shells, fighting over hiding holes or mates. They can communicate by drumming or flapping their pincers, which also serve to seize prey and dig.

ARROW CRAB
Stenorhynchus seticornis

COMMON EDIBLE CRAB
Cancer pagurus

GAUDY CLOWN CRAB
Platypodiella spectabilis

CORRUGATED CRAB
Liomera rugata

COMMON HAIRY CRAB
Pilumnus vespertilio

CANDY CRAB
Hoplophrys oatesii

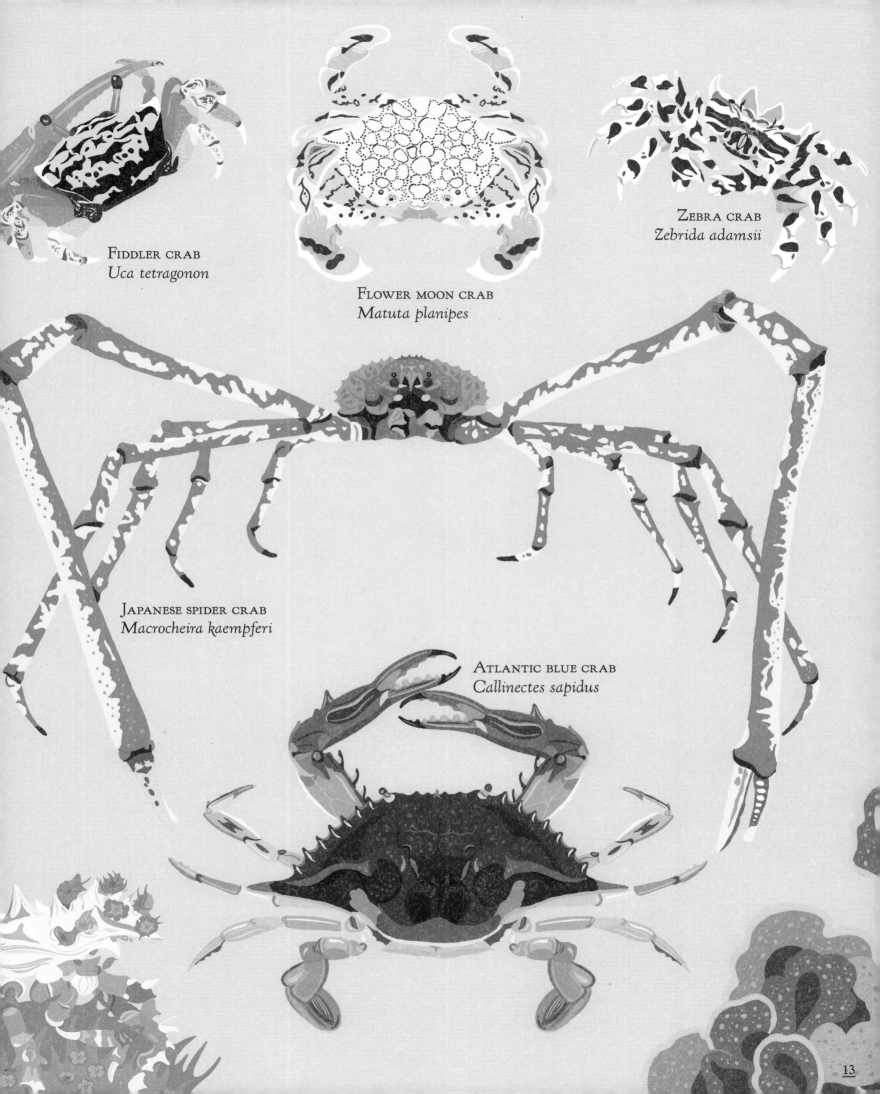

FIDDLER CRAB
Uca tetragonon

FLOWER MOON CRAB
Matuta planipes

ZEBRA CRAB
Zebrida adamsii

JAPANESE SPIDER CRAB
Macrocheira kaempferi

ATLANTIC BLUE CRAB
Callinectes sapidus

Hermit crabs

There are more than 1,000 species of these remarkable soft-bellied relatives of lobsters. They live in colonies on tropical shorelines and in shallow coral reefs, as well as on cooler coasts and in the deep sea. They work together to trade homes or find food, and can be found piled up on top of one another when they sleep.

A new home

It is a constant house search for a hermit crab. At any given time, 30 per cent of them are living in shells that are simply too small for them. They are always on the lookout for a larger home, combing the beaches and shallows for suitable 'properties' to move into.

COMMON HERMIT CRAB
Pagurus bernhardus

Sea anemones are useful bodyguards for hermit crabs, warding off predators with their stinging tentacles. Often the crabs attach anemones to their shells and carefully move them to any new shell that they adopt.

BLUEBERRY HERMIT CRAB
Coenobita purpureus

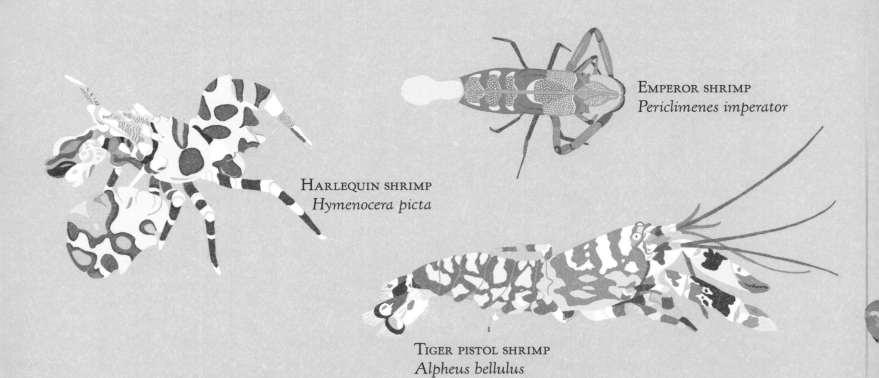

HARLEQUIN SHRIMP
Hymenocera picta

EMPEROR SHRIMP
Periclimenes imperator

TIGER PISTOL SHRIMP
Alpheus bellulus

SCARLET SKUNK CLEANER SHRIMP
Lysmata amboinensis

Shrimps and lobsters

Feeling their way with alien-like antennae, shrimps swim while lobsters mainly crawl or walk. These colourful crustaceans are related to crabs but are longer and more streamlined. Many use their claws to deadly effect – in the case of the pistol shrimp, to shoot out bullets of bubbles that stun its prey.

HONEYCOMB MORAY EEL
Gymnothorax favigeneus

The honeycomb moray eel and the cleaner shrimp have a great relationship. The tiny shrimp feeds on the parasites that could harm the larger animal. The shrimp searches all over, even inside the eel's mouth.

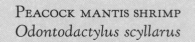

PEACOCK MANTIS SHRIMP
Odontodactylus scyllarus

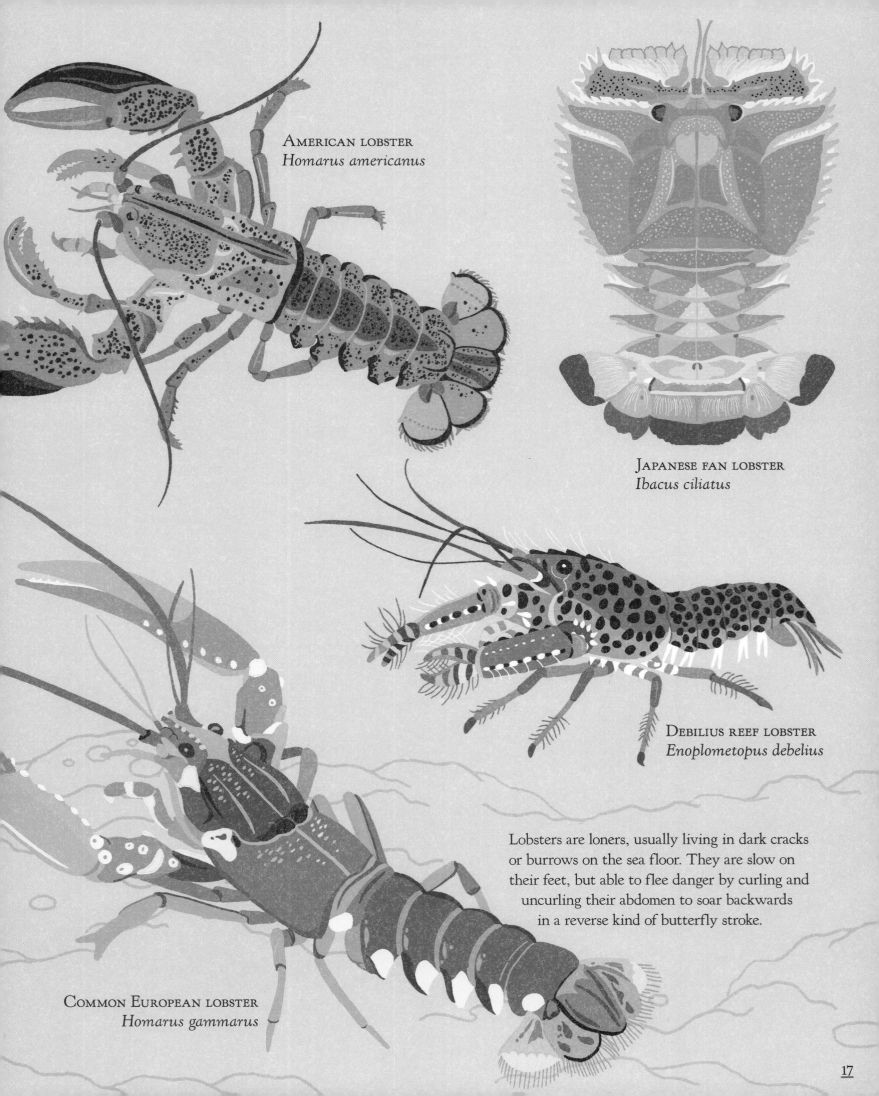

AMERICAN LOBSTER
Homarus americanus

JAPANESE FAN LOBSTER
Ibacus ciliatus

DEBILIUS REEF LOBSTER
Enoplometopus debelius

Lobsters are loners, usually living in dark cracks or burrows on the sea floor. They are slow on their feet, but able to flee danger by curling and uncurling their abdomen to soar backwards in a reverse kind of butterfly stroke.

COMMON EUROPEAN LOBSTER
Homarus gammarus

Sea stars

They have no head, blood or brain, but sea stars are survivors. If they lose an arm, they simply grow a new one; some can even regenerate from a broken limb. In an inside-out act, a sea star feeds by pushing its stomach out through its mouth. The sea star envelops the prey, digesting it, then sucks the stomach in again.

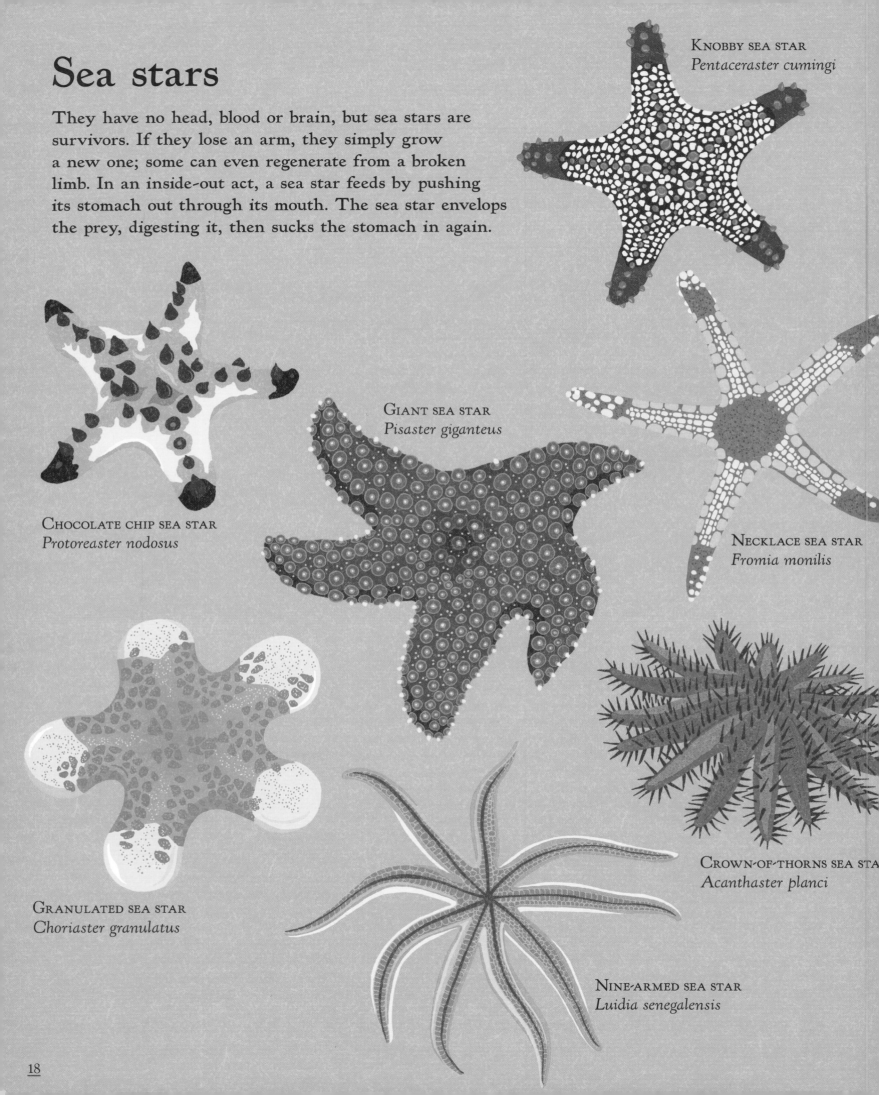

KNOBBY SEA STAR
Pentaceraster cumingi

CHOCOLATE CHIP SEA STAR
Protoreaster nodosus

GIANT SEA STAR
Pisaster giganteus

NECKLACE SEA STAR
Fromia monilis

GRANULATED SEA STAR
Choriaster granulatus

CROWN-OF-THORNS SEA STAR
Acanthaster planci

NINE-ARMED SEA STAR
Luidia senegalensis

Sea urchins

Like their sea star relatives, these spiny symmetrical creatures creep around on suckered feet. Their super-sharp teeth can drill hidey-holes in rock, while some species, such as the flower urchin, have a deadly venomous sting.

SPINY CUSHION STAR
Culcita schmideliana

SPUTNIK URCHIN
Phyllacanthus imperialis

SPINY BRITTLE STAR
Ophiothrix spiculata

NAKED BASKET STAR
Astroboa nuda

FIRE URCHIN
Astropyga radiata

FLOWER URCHIN
Toxopneustes pileolus

COMMON SEA URCHIN
Echinus esculentus

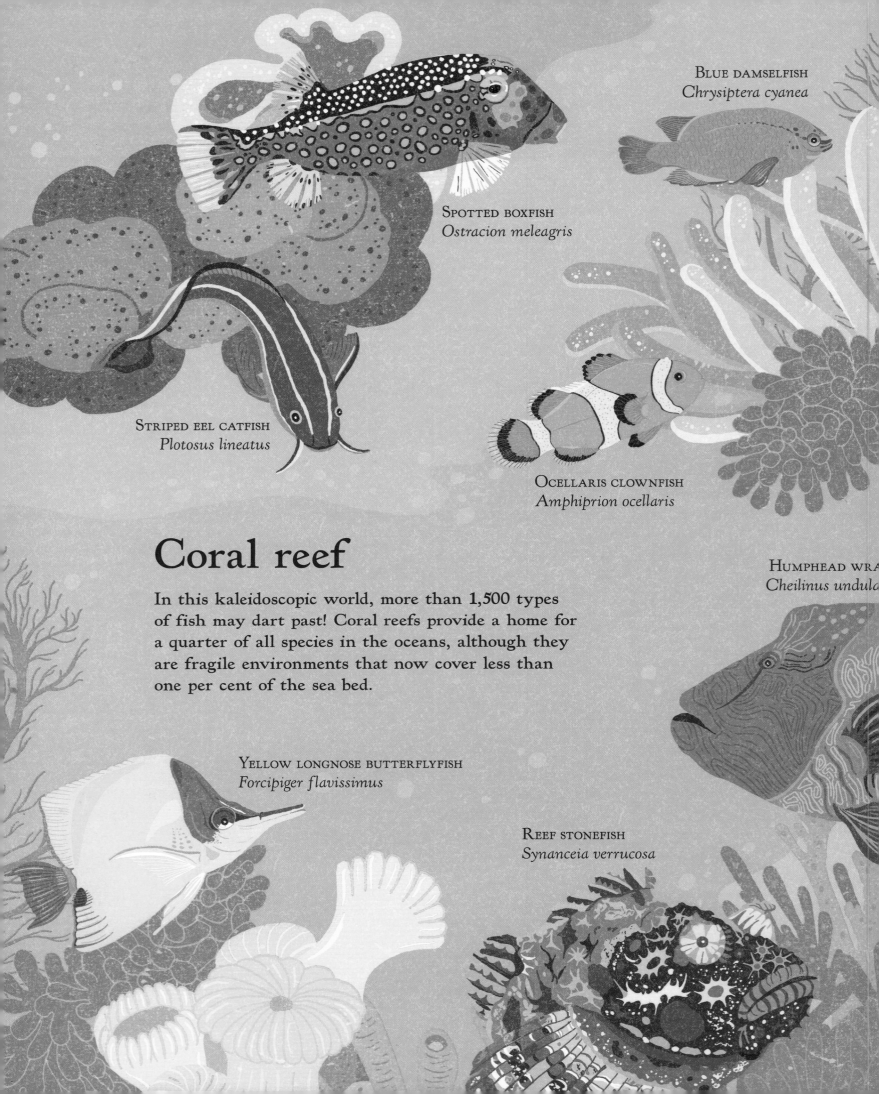

BLUE DAMSELFISH
Chrysiptera cyanea

SPOTTED BOXFISH
Ostracion meleagris

STRIPED EEL CATFISH
Plotosus lineatus

OCELLARIS CLOWNFISH
Amphiprion ocellaris

Coral reef

In this kaleidoscopic world, more than 1,500 types of fish may dart past! Coral reefs provide a home for a quarter of all species in the oceans, although they are fragile environments that now cover less than one per cent of the sea bed.

HUMPHEAD WRA
Cheilinus undula

YELLOW LONGNOSE BUTTERFLYFISH
Forcipiger flavissimus

REEF STONEFISH
Synanceia verrucosa

LAGOON TRIGGERFISH
Rhinecanthus aculeatus

JUVENILE EMPEROR ANGELFISH
Pomacanthus imperator

GREEN MANDARIN GOBY
Pterosynchiropus splendidus

BANDED SEA KRAIT
Laticauda colubrina

RED FIRE GOBY
Nemateleotris magnifica

POM-POM CRAB
Lybia edmondsoni

ROYAL ANGELFISH
Pygoplites diacanthus

RANDALL'S SHRIMP GOBY
Amblyeleotris randalli

Corals

Tiny, soft-bodied animals called polyps are the amazing architects that build a coral reef. They mass together in wonderfully shaped colonies, producing stony skeletons that fuse into rock-like forms. Coral reefs can grow for thousands of years as new polyps sprout on top of old ones.

BUBBLE CORAL
Plerogyra sinuosa

STAGHORN CORAL
Acropora cervicornis

PURPLE SEA FAN
Gorgonia ventalina

CARNATION TREE CORAL
Dendronephthya species

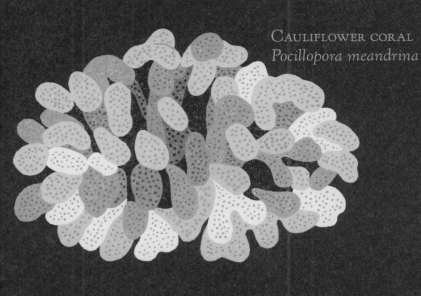

CAULIFLOWER CORAL
Pocillopora meandrina

SEA PEN
Pennatulacea species

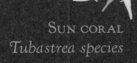

SUN CORAL
Tubastrea species

Some corals are soft and look a lot like plants, but all corals are animals. Tropical reef-building corals rely mainly on food made by algae that live in the polyps, giving them their brilliant colours. Because the algae need sunlight to thrive, corals bloom in warm, clear, shallow waters in the tropics.

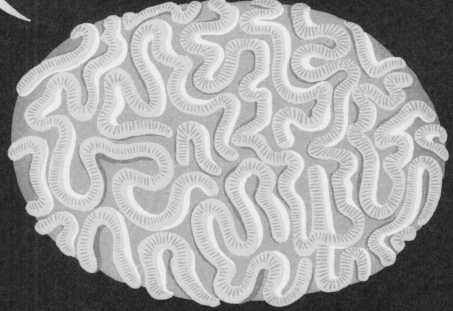

BRAIN CORAL
Diploria labyrinthiformis

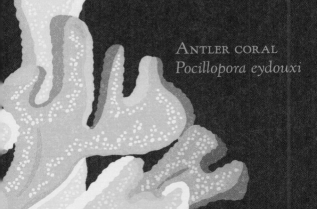

ANTLER CORAL
Pocillopora eydouxi

TOADSTOOL CORAL
Sarcophyton species

23

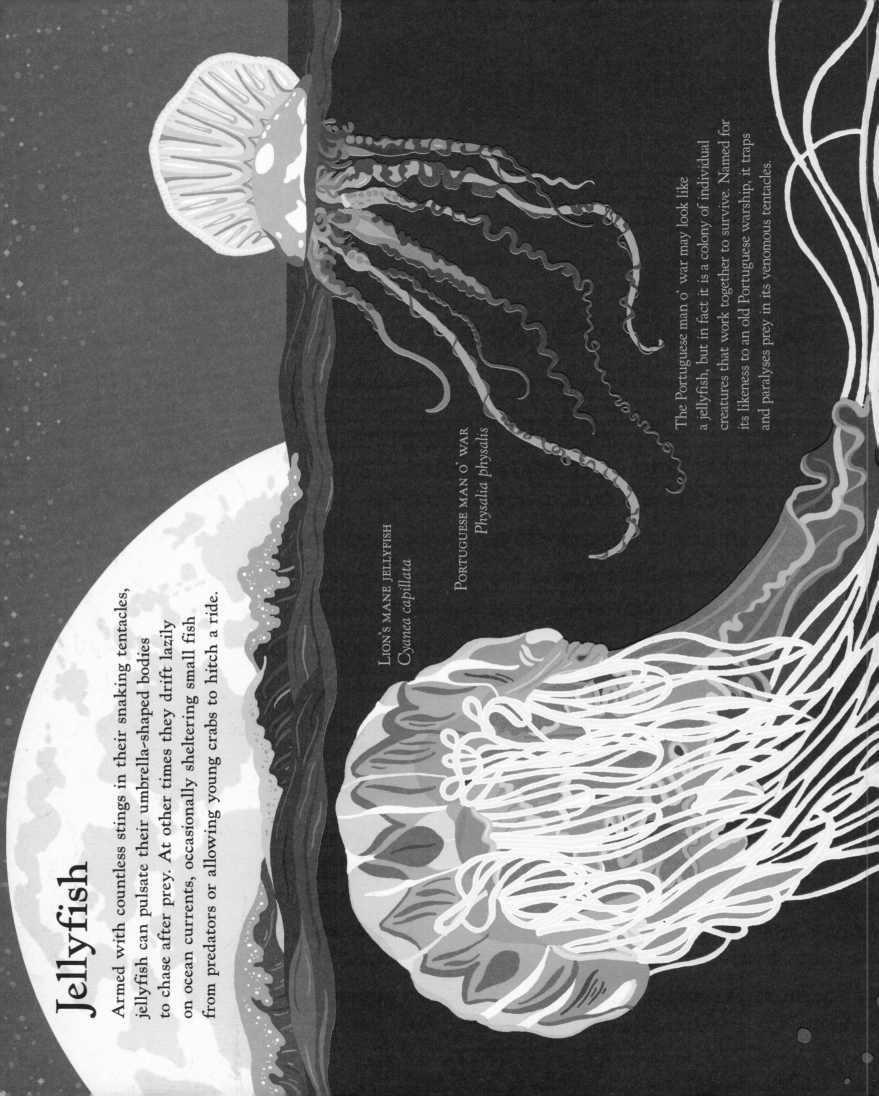

Jellyfish

Armed with countless stings in their snaking tentacles, jellyfish can pulsate their umbrella-shaped bodies to chase after prey. At other times they drift lazily on ocean currents, occasionally sheltering small fish from predators or allowing young crabs to hitch a ride.

LION'S MANE JELLYFISH
Cyanea capillata

PORTUGUESE MAN O' WAR
Physalia physalis

The Portuguese man o' war may look like a jellyfish, but in fact it is a colony of individual creatures that work together to survive. Named for its likeness to an old Portuguese warship, it traps and paralyses prey in its venomous tentacles.

CRYSTAL JELLY
Aequorea victoria

CAULIFLOWER JELLYFISH
Cephea cephea

ATOLLA JELLYFISH
Atolla wyvillei

MAUVE STINGER
Pelagia noctiluca

FRIED EGG JELLYFISH
Cotylorhiza tuberculata

UPSIDE-DOWN JELLYFISH
Cassiopea andromeda

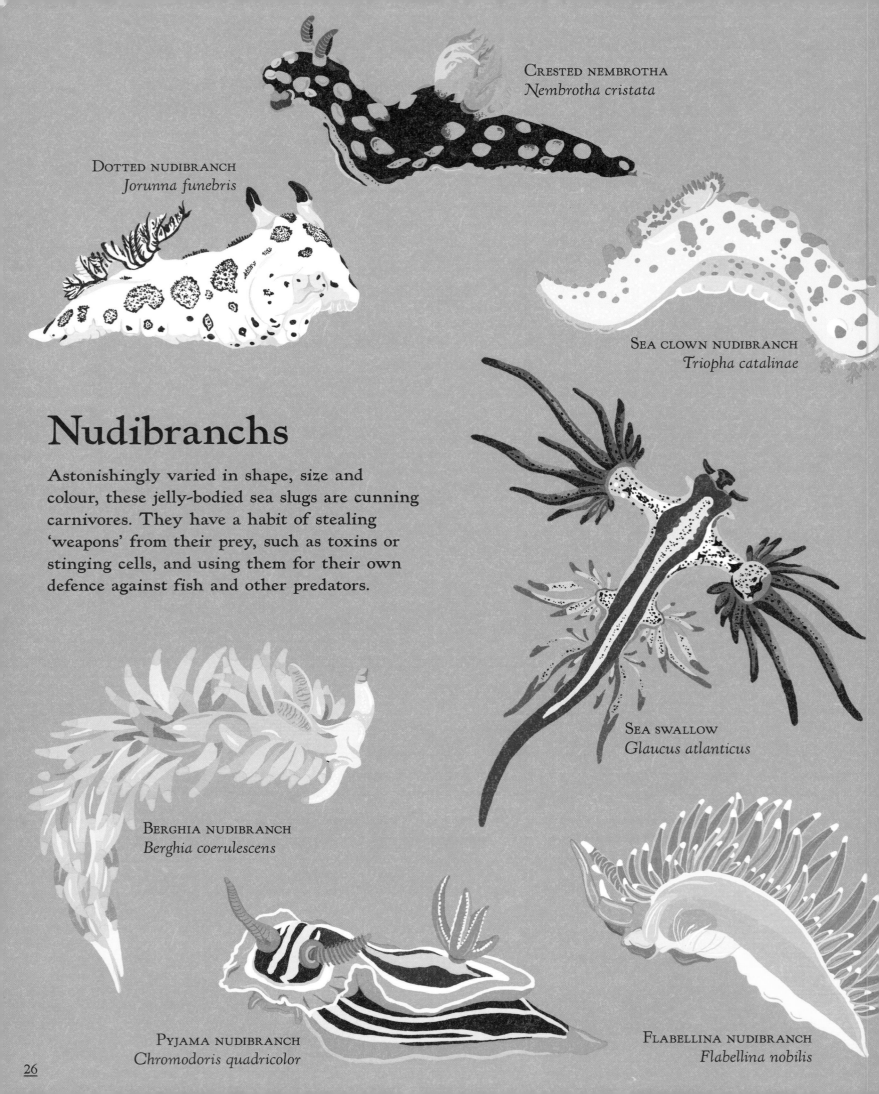

CRESTED NEMBROTHA
Nembrotha cristata

DOTTED NUDIBRANCH
Jorunna funebris

SEA CLOWN NUDIBRANCH
Triopha catalinae

Nudibranchs

Astonishingly varied in shape, size and colour, these jelly-bodied sea slugs are cunning carnivores. They have a habit of stealing 'weapons' from their prey, such as toxins or stinging cells, and using them for their own defence against fish and other predators.

SEA SWALLOW
Glaucus atlanticus

BERGHIA NUDIBRANCH
Berghia coerulescens

PYJAMA NUDIBRANCH
Chromodoris quadricolor

FLABELLINA NUDIBRANCH
Flabellina nobilis

SEA BUTTERFLY
Limacina helicina

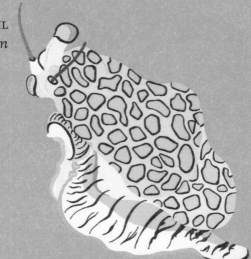

JEWELLED TOPSNAIL
Calliostoma annulatum

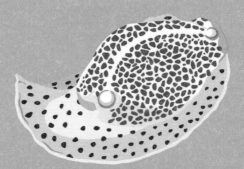

VENUS COMB MUREX
Murex pecten

WARTY EGG COWRY
Calpurnus verrucosus

Sea snails

A sea snail's armour is the shell on its back, which grows from a cloak-like mantle. Some species can swiftly wrap the mantle around their shell, like a change of clothes, to mystify predators. They are often tiny, some less than 1mm at adult size. Unlike their nudibranch cousins, some sea snails are herbivores.

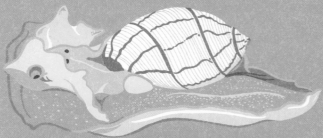

RED-LINED BUBBLE SNAIL
Bullina lineata

MOON SNAIL
Naticarius orientalis

INDIAN VOLUTE
Melo melo

Clams and bivalves

These soft-bodied molluscs lurk in hinged shells, often burrowing for extra safety into sand or rock. Some, such as scallops, clap their shells to swim, while cockles can jump by bending and flexing their muscular 'foot'. Most bivalves are filter-feeders, sifting tiny morsels from the water.

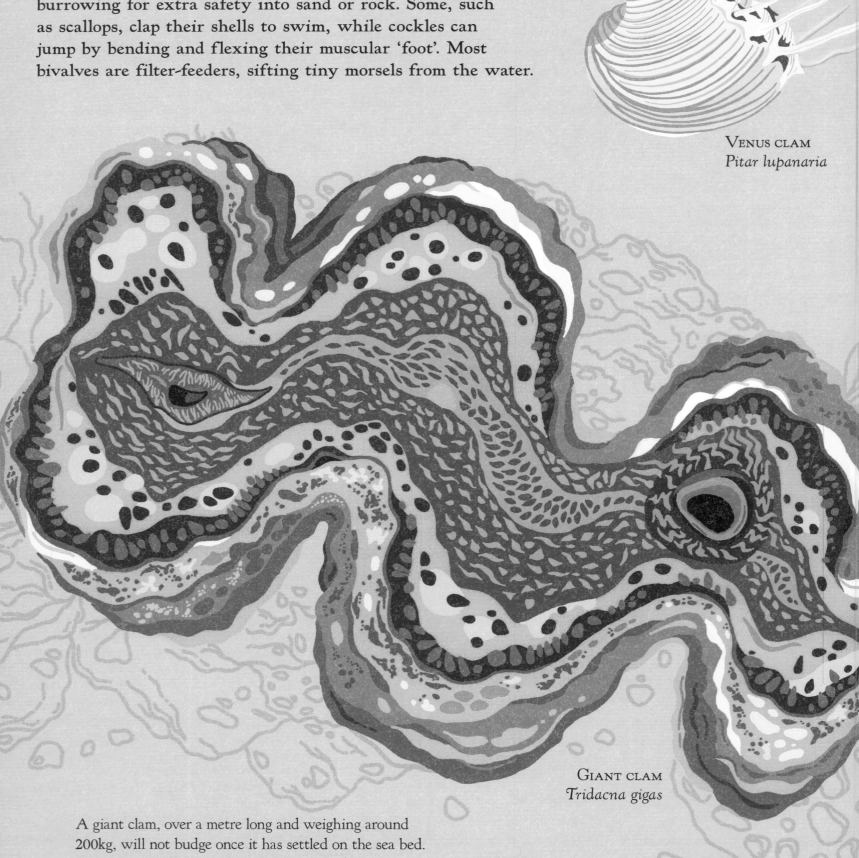

VENUS CLAM
Pitar lupanaria

GIANT CLAM
Tridacna gigas

A giant clam, over a metre long and weighing around 200kg, will not budge once it has settled on the sea bed. It can survive for more than 100 years, feeding on nutrients produced by algae that live in its mantle.

ATLANTIC JACKKNIFE CLAM
Ensis directus

GREAT SCALLOP
Pecten maximus

BLACK-LIP PEARL OYSTER
Pinctada margaritifera

BANDED VENUS CLAM
Clausinella fasciata

ZIGZAG VENUS CLAM
Lioconcha castrensis

BLUE MUSSEL
Mytilus edulis

FLORIDA PRICKLY COCKLE
Trachycardium egmontianum

Indonesian mimic octopus

Thaumoctopus mimicus

Few creatures on Earth have such extraordinary powers of camouflage as the mimic octopus. This marine magician can impersonate other animals by shape-shifting and changing its behaviour. Native to the warm coastal waters of Indonesia, it neatly tailors its disguise according to the predators around.

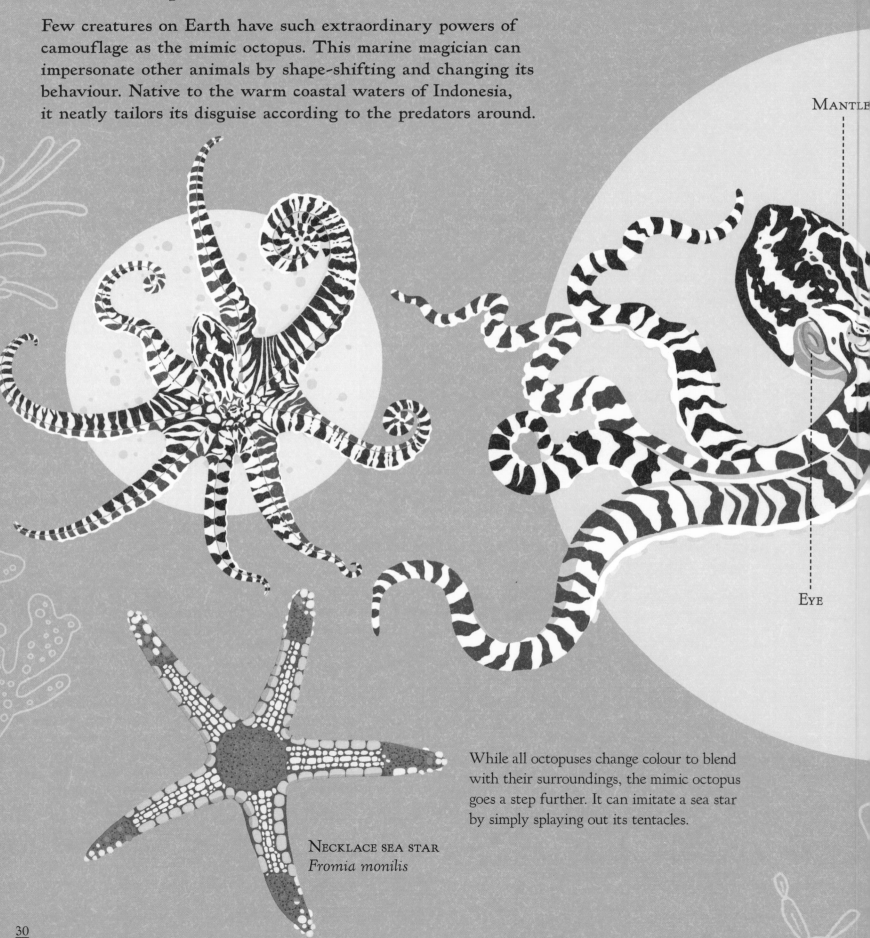

MANTLE

EYE

While all octopuses change colour to blend with their surroundings, the mimic octopus goes a step further. It can imitate a sea star by simply splaying out its tentacles.

NECKLACE SEA STAR
Fromia monilis

Lurking in a hole with only one of its tentacles poking out, the octopus puts off predators by its resemblance to a deadly banded sea snake!

BANDED SEA KRAIT
Laticauda colubrina

TENTACLE

The mimic octopus can swim along unthreatened if it pretends to be a large, rigid fish like a flounder.

SUCTION CUP

EYED FLOUNDER
Bothus ocellatus

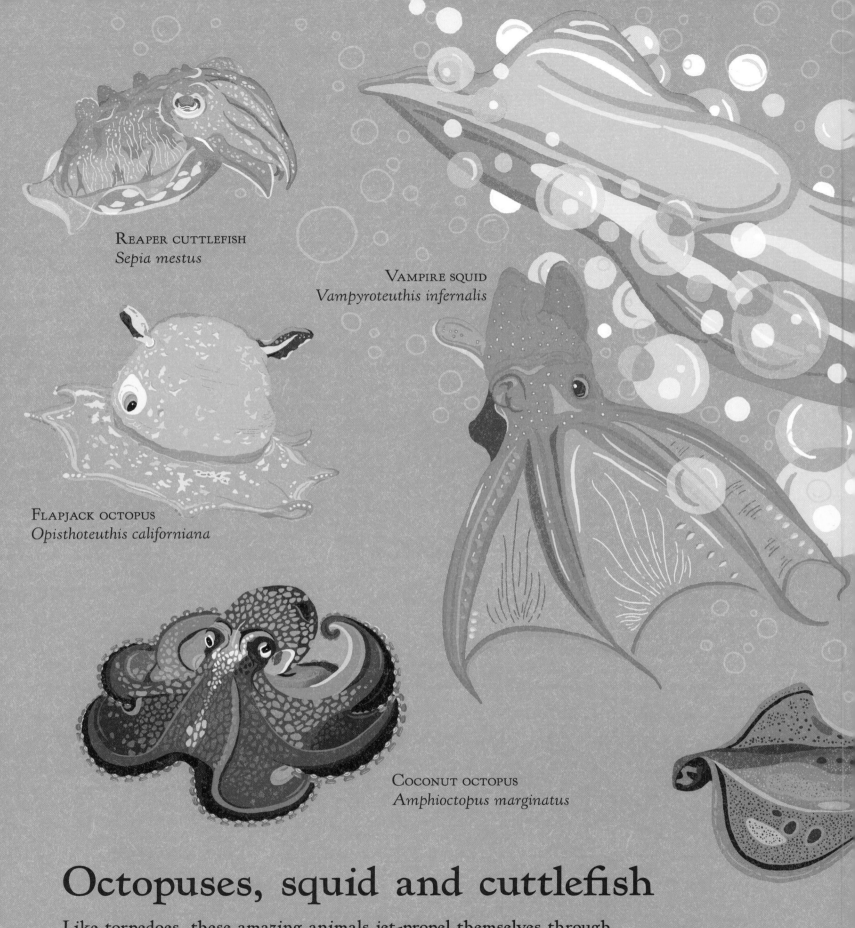

REAPER CUTTLEFISH
Sepia mestus

VAMPIRE SQUID
Vampyroteuthis infernalis

FLAPJACK OCTOPUS
Opisthoteuthis californiana

COCONUT OCTOPUS
Amphioctopus marginatus

Octopuses, squid and cuttlefish

Like torpedoes, these amazing animals jet-propel themselves through
the ocean, drawing water into their bodies, then blasting it out again.
Cephalopods, as these intelligent creatures are collectively known,
use their eight suckered tentacles for crawling and grabbing. In addition,
squid and cuttlefish have two further tentacles for snatching food.

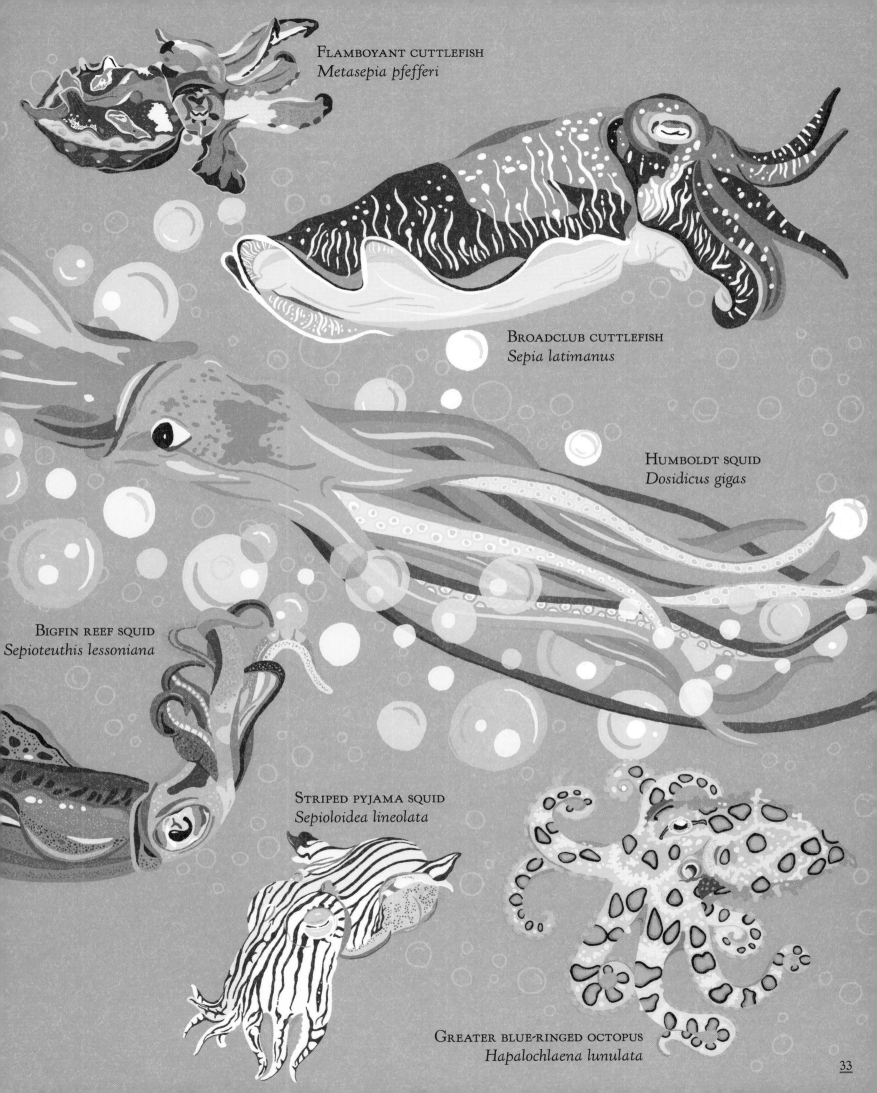

FLAMBOYANT CUTTLEFISH
Metasepia pfefferi

BROADCLUB CUTTLEFISH
Sepia latimanus

HUMBOLDT SQUID
Dosidicus gigas

BIGFIN REEF SQUID
Sepioteuthis lessoniana

STRIPED PYJAMA SQUID
Sepioloidea lineolata

GREATER BLUE-RINGED OCTOPUS
Hapalochlaena lunulata

Seahorses, seadragons and pipefish

They resemble mythical creatures with elegant equine snouts, but seahorses and their relatives, seadragons and pipefish, are all fish. Slow swimmers yet deadly predators, they blend in perfect camouflage with ocean weeds and corals to stealthily ambush their prey.

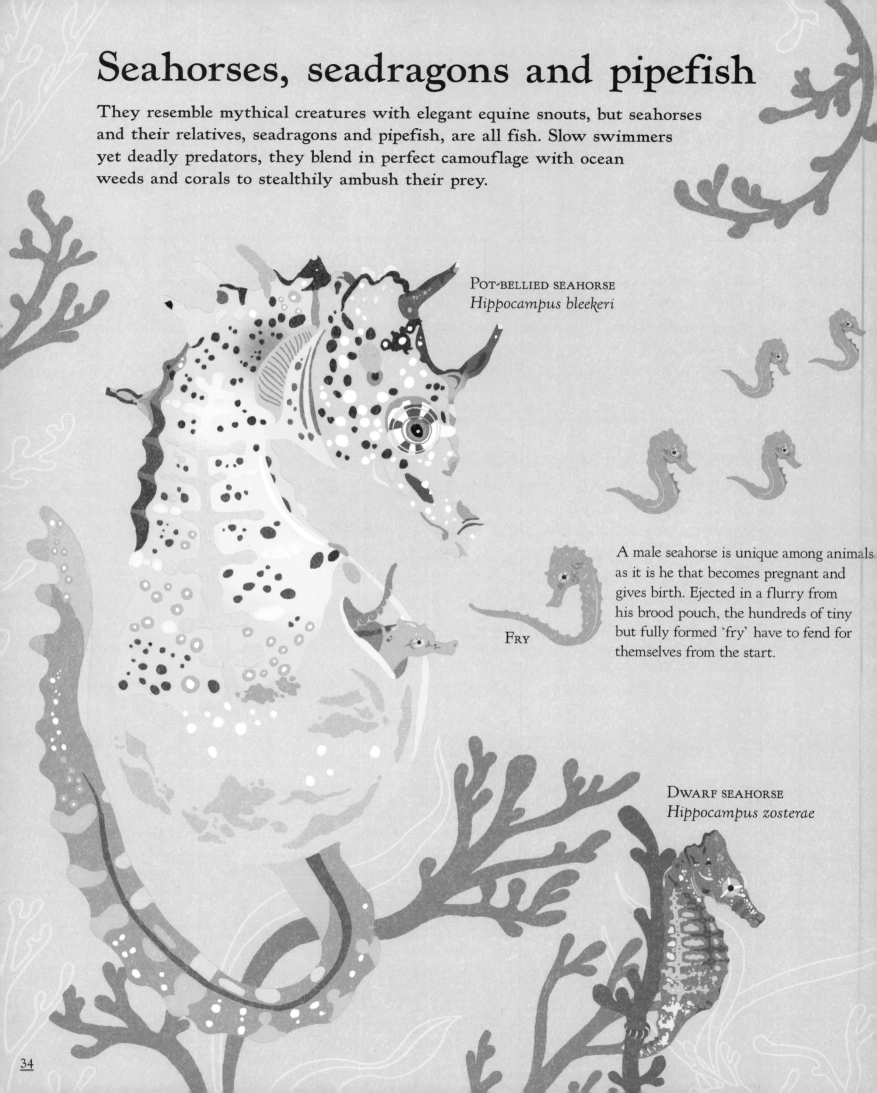

POT-BELLIED SEAHORSE
Hippocampus bleekeri

FRY

A male seahorse is unique among animals as it is he that becomes pregnant and gives birth. Ejected in a flurry from his brood pouch, the hundreds of tiny but fully formed 'fry' have to fend for themselves from the start.

DWARF SEAHORSE
Hippocampus zosterae

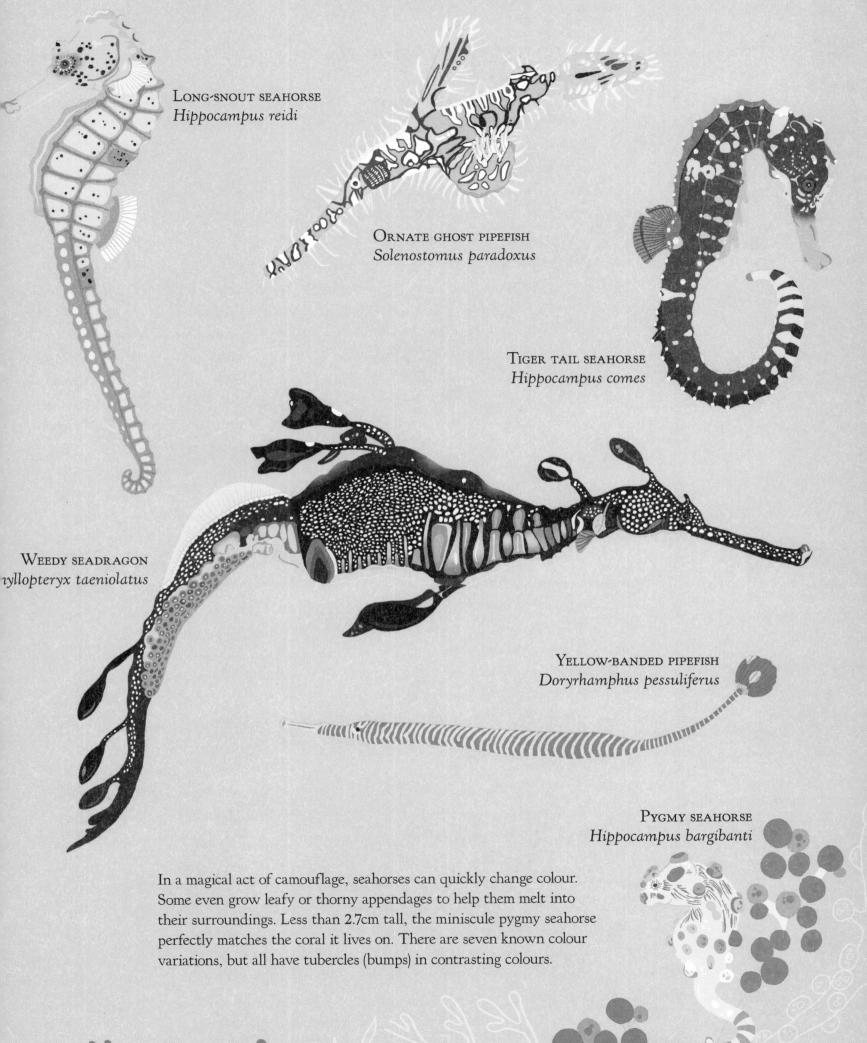

LONG-SNOUT SEAHORSE
Hippocampus reidi

ORNATE GHOST PIPEFISH
Solenostomus paradoxus

TIGER TAIL SEAHORSE
Hippocampus comes

WEEDY SEADRAGON
ꜱyllopteryx taeniolatus

YELLOW-BANDED PIPEFISH
Doryrhamphus pessuliferus

PYGMY SEAHORSE
Hippocampus bargibanti

In a magical act of camouflage, seahorses can quickly change colour. Some even grow leafy or thorny appendages to help them melt into their surroundings. Less than 2.7cm tall, the miniscule pygmy seahorse perfectly matches the coral it lives on. There are seven known colour variations, but all have tubercles (bumps) in contrasting colours.

Pufferfish and porcupinefish

A small, slow pufferfish sights a predator heading towards it and quickly gulps in huge mouthfuls of water. In an instant, its stomach stretches, inflating the fish to over twice its normal size. Now it does not look like such a tempting snack!

CHECKERED PUFFER
Sphoeroides testudineus

GOLDEN PUFFER
Arothron meleagris

VALENTIN'S SHARPNOSED PUFFER
Canthigaster valentini

Spot-fin porcupinefish
Diodon hystrix

If an attacker manages a bite before the pufferfish swells, there are still nasty shocks in store. Most puffers contain a powerful toxin that tastes vile and can be deadly. They also have tough, prickly skin. As an extra defence, porcupinefish are covered in long, sharp spines that stand up when the fish inflates.

Striped burrfish
Chilomycterus schoepfi

Globefish
Diodon nichthemerus

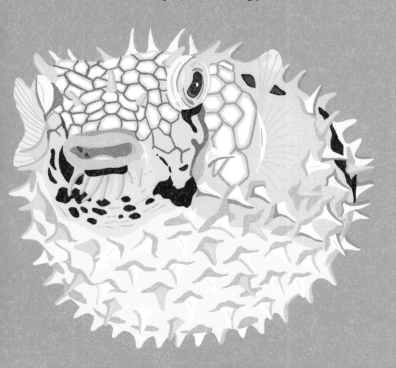

Swordfish v mackerel

There is frenzy in the open ocean as a ravenous swordfish strikes. Thrashing its razor-sharp bill from side to side, it sends a school of mackerel into panic mode. The attacker swims on through and out of the frantic mass of fish, but soon it will swoop back to devour any stunned or injured victims.

SWORDFISH
Xiphias gladius

The fast, agile swordfish swims alone, streamlined and rippling with muscle. It can track high-speed prey with a high-tech trick – it heats up its eyes to improve its vision. The adult swordfish has no teeth, so must slash prey with its sword or swallow it whole.

ATLANTIC MACKEREL
Scomber scombrus

Mackerel move quickly in co-ordinated schools, relying
on safety in numbers. With stripes on their backs
as markers, they can match each other's speed and
direction and so swim in perfect formation.

Sawfish, skates and rays

These close relatives of sharks creep around on the sea bed, watching the life going on above them through eyes on the tops of their heads. Flat-bodied and camouflaged, they are perfectly equipped to ambush their prey. Some deliver a powerful electric shock that stuns, while a stingray lashes out with a barbed sting near the end of its tail.

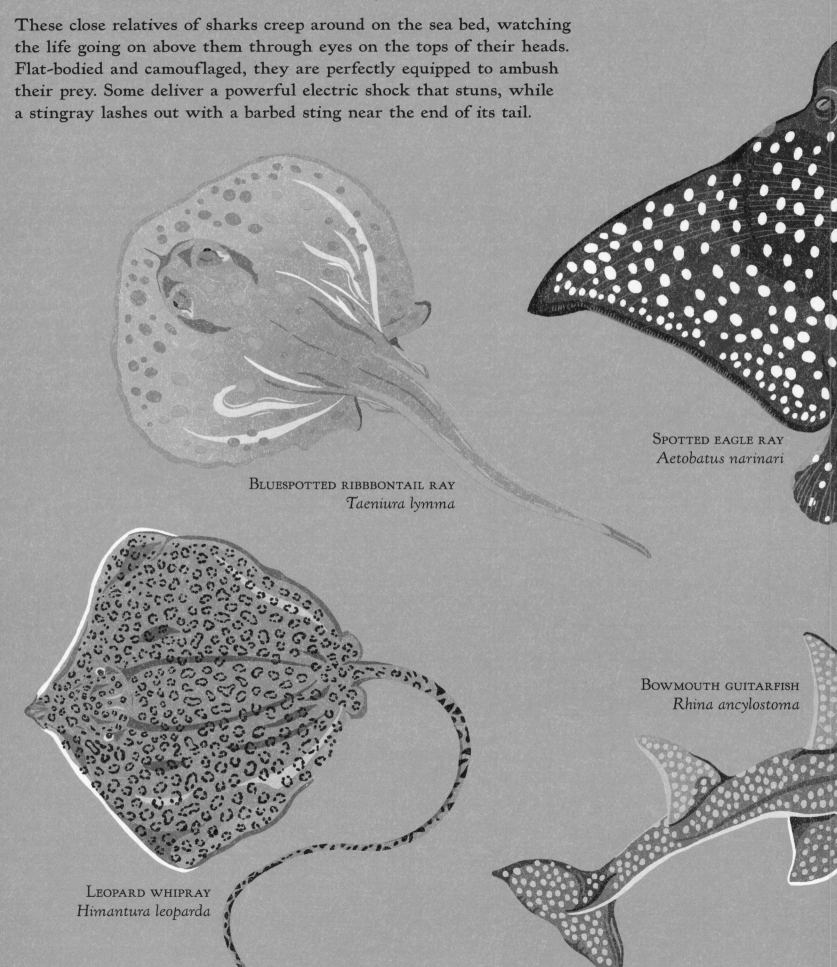

SPOTTED EAGLE RAY
Aetobatus narinari

BLUESPOTTED RIBBBONTAIL RAY
Taeniura lymma

BOWMOUTH GUITARFISH
Rhina ancylostoma

LEOPARD WHIPRAY
Himantura leoparda

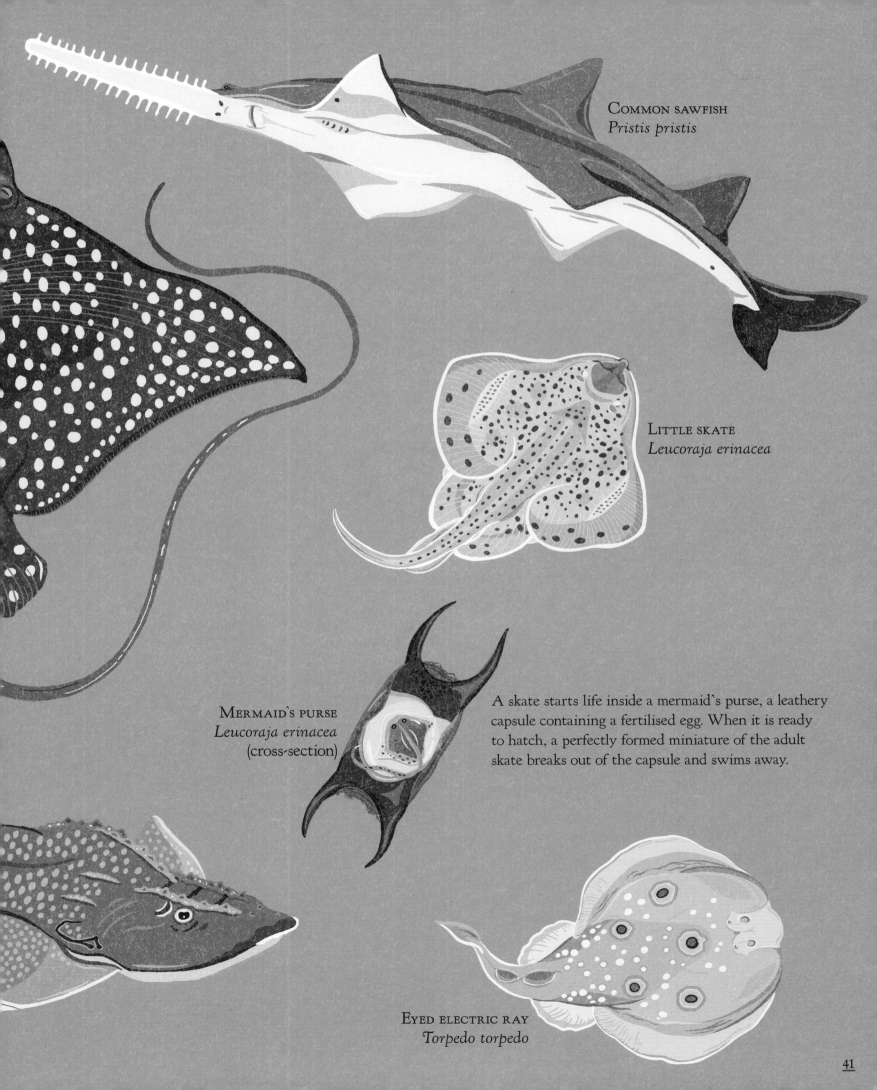

COMMON SAWFISH
Pristis pristis

LITTLE SKATE
Leucoraja erinacea

MERMAID'S PURSE
Leucoraja erinacea
(cross-section)

A skate starts life inside a mermaid's purse, a leathery capsule containing a fertilised egg. When it is ready to hatch, a perfectly formed miniature of the adult skate breaks out of the capsule and swims away.

EYED ELECTRIC RAY
Torpedo torpedo

Sharks

Sharks prowl the oceans wherever there is life, armed with acute senses and precision jaws. There are more than 400 species of these intelligent fish. Their superpower is an extreme 'sixth sense', which detects tiny electrical pulses in their prey. Most sharks are hunters, tactical and fast, but the biggest thrive by sucking in plankton.

Remoras are known as 'sharksuckers' for a reason – they ride around on sharks and other marine animals. As they cling on, they snatch stray scraps from the sharks' food.

BASKING SHARK
Cetorhinus maximus

BULL SHARK
Carcharhinus leucas

ZEBRA BULLHEAD SHARK
Heterodontus zebra

WHALE SHARK
Rhincodon typus

BLUE SHARK
Prionace glauca

GREAT HAMMERHEAD
Sphyrna mokarran

FRILLED SHARK
Chlamydoselachus anguineus

SPOTTED WOBBEGONG
Orectolobus maculatus

43

ORCA
Orcinus orca

Both of these animals are apex predators, at the top of the ocean food web. Able to smell a drop of blood in a billion drops of water, the great white shark is a fearsome fish. Orcas, a type of dolphin, are bigger and faster. When they hunt together, they are rarely defeated in a fight.

Orcas v great white shark

Two titanic terrors of the ocean size each other up for battle. The great white shark, all jaws and teeth, is challenged by a pack of hungry orcas. The orcas gang up to exhaust and outwit their prey, but the shark is packed with power. Who will win?

GREAT WHITE SHARK
Carcharodon carcharias

Dolphins

Graceful, streamlined dolphins can leap high out of the water or plunge down deep. These intelligent, social mammals live and travel in groups called pods, hunting together and sharing the care of their young. To communicate they let out a series of chirps and whistles, but they also make clicking sounds to echolocate and catch their prey, before swallowing it whole.

ATLANTIC SPOTTED DOLPHIN
Stenella frontalis

RISSO'S DOLPHIN
Grampus griseus

COMMERSON'S DOLPHIN
Cephalorhynchus commersonii

COMMON BOTTLENOSE DOLPHIN
Tursiops truncatus

ATLANTIC WHITE-SIDED DOLPHIN
Lagenorhynchus acutus

CHINESE WHITE DOLPHIN
Sousa chinensis

SPINNER DOLPHIN
Stenella longirostris

Whales

The giants of the ocean are whales – graceful mammals with blubber-wrapped bodies and haunting calls that ripple far and wide. They offer some of nature's most spectacular sights, from a mighty humpback leaping out of the water to the colossal blue whale, bigger than even the largest dinosaurs.

BELUGA WHALE
Delphinapterus leucas

HUMPBACK WHALE
Megaptera novaeangliae

BLUE WHALE
Balaenoptera musculus

SOUTHERN RIGHT WHALE
Eubalaena australis

STRAP-TOOTHED WHALE
Mesoplodon layardii

SPERM WHALE
Physeter macrocephalus

A whale needs to surface regularly to breathe air through the blowholes on its head. The sperm whale has a remarkable ability to hold its breath for longer than the rest, making deep dives that can last for up to 90 minutes.

Turtles

Ancient enough to have swum with prehistoric fish, marine turtles have been cruising the world's oceans for more than 100 million years. These swift, shelled reptiles are expert navigators, swimming thousands of kilometres between their feeding and nesting grounds, and amazingly are able to find the way back to the beach where they were born to lay their eggs.

The leatherback is the champion of turtles, growing the largest and swimming the furthest and fastest. It can plunge down 1,000m and stay underwater for several hours, chasing jellyfish as its almost exclusive prey.

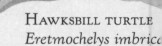

HAWKSBILL TURTLE
Eretmochelys imbrica

LEATHERBACK TURTLE
Dermochelys coriacea

FLATBACK SEA TURTLE
Natator depressus

KEMP'S RIDLEY TURTLE
Lepidochelys kempii

While adult male turtles never leave the ocean, females come ashore to lay their eggs in the sand before returning to the sea. Their newly hatched young face a risky journey, with predators lurking as they dig themselves out of the sand and make their way unsteadily to the water.

LOGGERHEAD TURTLE
Caretta caretta

Dugongs
Dugong dugon

This vegetarian relative of the elephant grazes languidly on seagrass in shallow ocean meadows, both by day and by night. Rooting around with its sensitive bristled snout, it must surface every few minutes to breathe. The dugong is the only herbivorous marine mammal and has earned the nickname 'sea cow' thanks to its never-ending appetite for grass.

Sea otters
Enhydra lutris

Making short dives to the ocean floor, the sea otter hunts its prey, then swims up for air. Crack! It breaks the shell of a spiny sea urchin on a rock held on its chest. While eating its tasty morsel, the otter lounges on the water's surface. It has a unique habit of wrapping itself in kelp to avoid drifting away while eating or during a snooze.

Seals, sealions and walruses

A thick layer of blubber insulates seals and their relatives as they plunge through chilly waters or bask on ice. Known as pinnipeds, meaning 'winged feet', these flippered mammals are graceful swimmers that spend most of their lives at sea. They are cumbersome on land but will haul themselves ashore to breed, escape predators, rest and moult.

CALIFORNIA SEA LION
Zalophus californianus

RINGED SEAL
Pusa hispida

The hulking male elephant seal lets out a loud roar to intimidate its rivals. The largest and heaviest of all the seals, it can wage a long and bloody battle to win a mate.

SOUTHERN ELEPHANT SEAL
Mirounga leonine

SPOTTED SEAL
Phoca largha

A walrus' long tusks are not just for fighting. They also make useful tools when it comes to clambering out of the water or breaking open breathing holes in ice.

HARP SEAL
Pagophilus groenlandicus

LEOPARD SEAL
Hydrurga leptonyx

WALRUS
Odobenus rosmarus

Penguins

These torpedo-shaped flightless birds are truly adaptable, mating and raising young on bare, rocky land and even ice, but spending most of their lives in the deep waters of the icy ocean. They are superb swimmers, using their short, stubby wings as flippers and surfacing regularly for air.

SOUTHERN ROCKHOPPER PENGUIN
Eudyptes chrysocome

ADÉLIE PENGUIN
Pygoscelis adeliae

CHINSTRAP PENGUIN
Pygoscelis antarcticus

LITTLE PENGUIN
Eudyptula minor

Penguins cannot fly in the air, but they certainly 'fly' through the water, twisting and turning rapidly in search of the fish, squid and tiny krill that they eat. Their heavy, dense bones help them to dive deep for food.

MACARONI PENGUIN JUVENILE
Eudyptes chrysolophus

YELLOW-EYED PENGUIN
Megadyptes antipodes

EMPEROR PENGUIN AND CHICK
Aptenodytes forsteri

GENTOO PENGUIN
Pygoscelis papua

HUMBOLDT PENGUIN
Spheniscus humboldti

ABYSSAL GHOSTSHARK
Hydrolagus trolli

Creatures of the deep

The largest habitat on Earth is an alien world, mostly unknown to humans. Pitch dark and under immense pressure from the weight of water above, the deep sea is home to a host of otherworldly creatures that use luminous organs, jelly-like bodies and other incredible adaptations to survive against the odds.

HELMET JELLYFISH
Periphylla periphylla

GIANT TUBE WORMS
Riftia bachyptila

BLOBFISH
Psychrolutes marcidus

ANGLERFISH
Caulophryne pelagica

GULPER EEL
Eurypharynx pelecanoides

TRIPODFISH
Bathypterois grallator

LYRE SPONGE
Chondrocladia lyra

VENT CRAB
Shinkaia crosnieri.

SOUTHERN OCEAN GIANT SEA SPIDER
Colossendeis megalonyx

Glossary

ALGAE — Organisms that range in size from single cells to large spreading seaweeds. They make their own food from sunlight and release oxygen into the water and atmosphere.

BIVALVE — Any mollusc, such as a mussel, that has two shells hinged together, a soft body and gills.

BLOWHOLE — The hole at the top of the head in whales and dolphins, through which they breathe.

BLUBBER — A thick layer of fatty tissue beneath the skin of aquatic mammals such as whales or seals.

BROOD POUCH — A pocket or cavity in male seahorses where eggs develop and hatch.

CAMOUFLAGE — The natural colouring or features that allow an animal to blend in with its surroundings.

CEPHALOPOD — Any of the group of sea animals, such as cuttlefish, squid and octopus, that have suckered tentacles attached to the head.

COLONIES — The communities of animals, such as hermit crabs or corals, that live together and interact with each other.

CRUSTACEANS — Animals that live mostly in water and have a hard shell and segmented body. Crustaceans include lobsters, crabs and shrimps.

ECHOLOCATE — To find objects by recognising the time it takes for an echo to return and the direction from which it comes.

FILTER-FEEDER — An ocean animal, such as a baleen whale, that feeds on particles or tiny organisms that it strains out of the water.

HERBIVORES — Animals that eat only plants.

INSULATES — Prevents heat escaping from the body.

MANTLE — A layer of soft tissue that covers the body of a clam, oyster or other mollusc, and exudes the material that forms the shell.

MOLLUSCS — A group of soft-bodied animals that live on land and in both fresh and saltwater. Molluscs include sea snails, mussels and clams.

MOULT — To shed skin to make way for new growth.

NUTRIENTS — Essential substances that feed and nourish animals.

PARASITE — An organism that lives on or in another species and takes nutrients from its host.

PINNIPEDS — A group of sea mammals that have fin-like flippers for swimming.

PLANKTON — Small, drifting plants and animals, such as microscopic algae and protozoa, that are a primary food source for many oceanic animals.

POD — A small group, for example of dolphins or whales.

POLYPS — Tiny animals that form coral colonies. Each polyp has its own feeding tentacles, but is attached to other polyps and shares nutrients with them.

PREDATORS — Animals that hunt and kill other animals for food.

PREY — Animals that are killed and eaten by other animals.

REEF — A ridge of coral, rocks or sand that rises near the surface of shallow seas.

SCHOOL — A large number of fish that feed or migrate together.

SPECIES — A type or group of living things with similar characteristics.

SPINE — A sharp-pointed, bony barb on a fish.

STREAMLINED — Having a shape that moves through water fast and efficiently.

TENTACLE — A narrow, unjointed part extending from the body of an animal, such as a jellyfish, that is used for feeling, grasping or moving.

TOXINS — Poisonous substances.

TUBERCLE — A small, rounded swelling, usually on the skin of an animal.

VENOMOUS — Equipped with a poisonous sting or fangs.

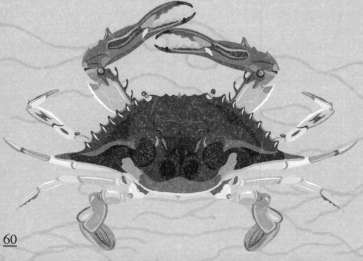

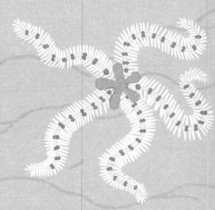

Index

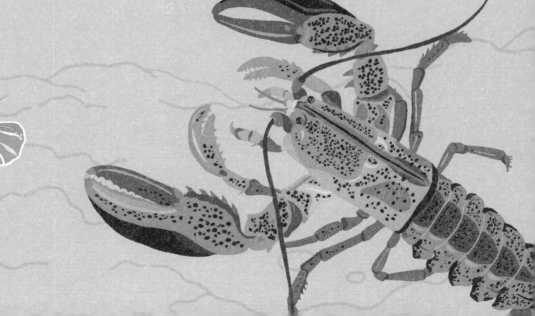